simple outdoor style

simple

outdoor

style

LJILJANA BAIRD

Photographs by Olivier Maynard

WATSON-GUPTILL PUBLICATIONS/NEW YORK

Acknowledgments

Many, many thanks to Malabar for generously providing fabrics for the projects,
and to Susan Marfleet for her swift and efficient dispatch of last-minute fabric requests.
Thanks also to Tricia Tucker and her team for realizing the design sketches.

Copyright © 1998 by MQ Publications, Ltd.
Text © 1998 by Ljiljana Baird
Photographs © 1998 by Olivier Maynard

Published by MQ Publications, Ltd.,
254–258 Goswell Road,
London EC1V 7EB
Series Editor: Ljiljana Baird
Editor: Simona Hill
Designer: Bet Ayer

First published in the United States in 1998
by Watson-Guptill Publications,
a division of BPI Communications, Inc.,
1515 Broadway, New York, N.Y. 10036

Library of Congress Catalog Card Number: 97-62230

ISBN 0-8230-4801-2

Printed in Italy

First printing, 1998

1 2 3 4 5 6 7 8 9 / 06 05 04 03 02 01 00 99 98

contents

◆

introduction

◆

Mention the word "outdoors" and we conjure up images of hiking across the countryside, camping in woods and forests, boating on lakes and rivers, and swimming and sailing on the sea. It suggests fresh air and space to be oneself. Outdoors can also encompass situations more domestic and closer to home: the local park, your own garden, and even a patio or balcony for those of us who live in apartments in a city environment. The outdoors carries notions of well-being, relaxation, challenging recreational activities, and places that are free from day-to-day pressures.

The outdoors offers physical and emotional escape from the enclosures and boundaries that prescribe our activities and behavior, whether we are at home, school, or work. I have always regarded it as the great release, the "breathe out." Watch children tumble out of class into the playground or from a bus on an outing—they squeal and roar and run with pleasure at the freedom. Even when our normal daily activities are happy and smooth-running, the outdoors offers a welcome recreational and relaxing change. But when life makes too many demands and we are desperate for relief from daily pressures, many of us like to take a brisk walk, work in the garden, or collapse on a beach. In short, we distance ourselves physically from the pressure and, in doing so, claw back a little space in which to assess and review our problems. The old-fashioned remedy of stepping out to take the air is not unlike current medical advice for healthy living—to get plenty of fresh

air and exercise. The fresh air blows the cobwebs away and encourages activities of a type that are usually enjoyable, and the element of fun in turn helps to relieve stress and the accompanying unattractive physical symptoms of our fast-track lifestyle.

The outdoors is a vital ingredient in a happy and healthy life. *Simple Outdoor Style* looks at projects that can enhance our enjoyment of this wonderful natural resource in the spring and summer months. Outdoor activities can be marred by too much sun and wind, irritating insects, uncomfortable seating, and inappropriate tableware.

The criteria proposed for each project considered for inclusion in this book were simplicity of design and construction, function, safety, attractiveness, ease of maintenance, portability, and availability and economy of materials. When a project answered positively to all these requirements, it was then included. A simple lifestyle is essentially about an easy, low-maintenance way of living, from which fuss and extraneous knick-knacks are removed to optimize time and space for priorities. But at the same time it pares down, simple style is observant of the visual appeal of what remains. We want to surround ourselves with objects in which function and style work together as one. With these objectives in mind, simple style still remains a personal approach. Readers will interpret the suggestions and guidelines within their own set of preferences and adapt the projects to best suit themselves.

The book is divided into five categories that roughly address the main aspects of domestic outdoor life: lounging, shade and shelter, eating, seating, and accessories. The projects have been designed in the simplest possible way to ensure that they are within every crafter's capabilities, using equipment, tools, and materials that can be found in their local craft, home improvement, or department store. Time and cost were also important considerations. Outdoor furniture and accessories must be reasonably robust to withstand the demands of the elements and our inattention. Since most of us are reluctant to put everything away at the first sign of wet weather, items get left out, and, within a few seasons, materials and fabrics perish. So if we are to replace or refurbish outdoor equipment, speed of construction should be considered. Replacing the fabric on a deck chair or folding picnic stools requires less than an hour's work; a set of six buttoned placemats can be sewn in a few hours;

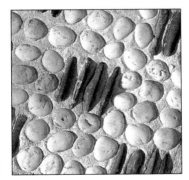

similarly, the garden candles, envelope cushion covers, and hammock can be made in a morning. Because I know that replacing any of the projects won't demand much of my time, I can relax about leaving them outside in wind and weather. Not being anxious about one's possessions is an important factor in a simple lifestyle. I am not suggesting that we be neglectful; rather, I'm suggesting that, with better planning and forethought about what we buy or make for our home, we can reduce our maintenance worries without sacrificing appearance. For example, you want the peace of mind that, should a guest spill something on a tablecloth, chair cover, or cushion, or if children drop ice cream on the hammock, the offending stains can be easily removed with a quick wash in the machine. So for convenience, choose fabrics that are readily available, inexpensive, and easy to clean. For all the sewing projects I have chosen natural fibers such as cotton and linen. These are ideal fabrics for the outdoors: they are available in a wide range of standard and fashion colors, they are machine washable, they press well and hang beautifully, and they are easy to handle when sewing. Being comfortable against the skin, they are especially suitable for hot weather and, unlike polyester- and nylon-based fabrics, do not as a rule cause skin irritation. These two fabrics also look good—natural-color or bleached linen or cotton are elegant. They

blend harmoniously with the colors of the outdoors. Beige-on-beige striped cotton fabric looks wonderful against the riotous colors of a summer garden and would look equally well on a beach, or against the greens of trees. In contrast, for other projects I have selected outrageously bright colors that compete with nature's own exuberant summer palette. The candy pink madras cotton director's chair cover sings as loudly as a colorful herbaceous border. Combining squares of orange and pink with lime green in a patch-work picnic blanket expresses the fun of outdoor living, as do the orange and yellow chosen for the two-color tablecloth and matching chair. Like bees, we are attracted to color—it lifts our spirits and provides nourishment of sorts.

I have avoided patterned fabrics, choosing for the projects solids or stripes, and in one instance a plaid. Patterns date, whereas classic stripes and plaids remain timeless and unobtrusive. They are also much easier to mix and match. Patterned fabrics are frequently too busy and distract from the function of the item. When thinking about your table linen, consider the color of your china and glassware; they need to enhance each other. I think the yellow wine glasses look superb against the natural-color linen of the beaded tablerunners on page 60—the colors invite you to the table which is the purpose of a table setting.

As you create the props for your outdoor life, keep in mind the function of each object; that way, you will ensure that your garden is full of furnishings that are are comfortable, practical, and desirable. If function is your guide, then attractiveness and simplicity of design and style will follow.

INTRODUCTION

shade and shelter

The past several years have seen a change in attitude toward sunbathing and, while we are encouraged to use the outdoors as another living space, we have also been advised of the long-term ill effects of prolonged exposure to sunlight, not to mention the immediate discomfort of sunburn. But at the same time we want to be stylish, not covered from head to toe, swamped in oversized T-shirts and full-brimmed hats. Outdoors is about looking good, but it is also about being comfortable and safe and having fun. To this end, this chapter offers four amazingly simple-to-make but stylish projects that provide shade and shelter and will appeal to everybody—a parasol tent that is large enough for a small tea party and doubles as a private outdoor reading room or elegant poolside changing booth; a beach awning suspended from long bamboo poles or in a woodland setting can be tied to the branches of trees; a heavenly white sheer canopy that protects against irritating insects, both indoors and outdoors; and a windbreak-cum-outdoor shower screen, complete with storage pockets for newspapers, sunblock, toothbrush, and comb.

I have chosen mainly neutral colors for all of the projects to allow them to rest quietly, look good, and blend in anywhere outdoors. All of the projects are portable and are designed to be used at home in the garden, on the beach, in the woods, by the swimming pool, on the riverbank, or in the park. For ease, choose fabrics and materials that are lightweight but strong and machine washable. These include strong woven natural fabrics such as canvas, cotton cambric, muslin, denim, chambray, ticking, drill, duck, khaki, oilcloth, and sailcloth. They must be able to stand the rigors of repeated handling.

If an item is a permanent summer fixture, choose neutral shades that will not fade in the sun, and pick fabrics strong enough to withstand the harshness of summer weather.

SHADE AND SHELTER

parasol
changing tent

◆

It was from watching my children fashion such successful and innovative "homes" from ordinary materials that the idea of a camp-style tent came to mind. On this occasion, it happened to be beach towels draped over an umbrella, which happily accommodated two children, dolls, and pets. A private hideaway, just for two, a tête-à-tête in the calm cool of the garden with the same ease of assembly appealed to me as well. In response I have come up with a design that requires no other skills than sewing a straight line. Using as my structure a sturdy white canvas market parasol, now a familiar sight on patios, balconies, and gardens, I simply attached eight panels of fabric to the rim of the umbrella. So that the tent can be easily brought in for the winter, I have chosen the simplest of fasteners—rings and ties. The panels are tied through rings to the parasol and the panels are tied together down the length. This method also allows you to roll up panels to increase light and ventilation.

▶ 15

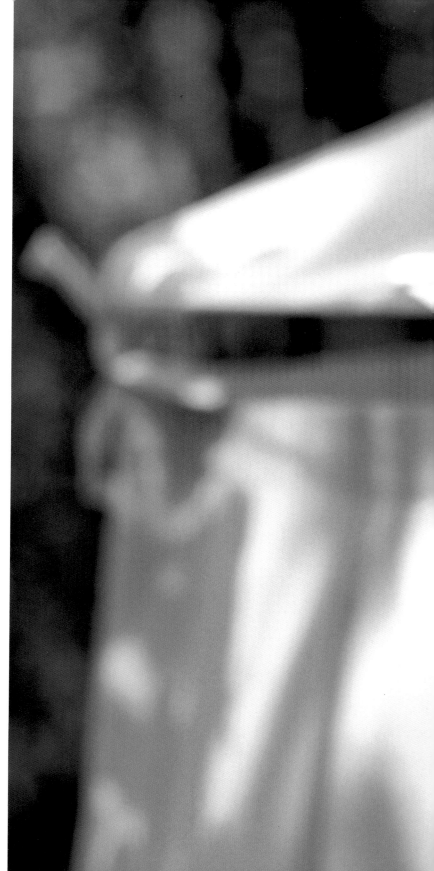

Ties and small brass rings make this tent easy to assemble and allow individual panels to be rolled up as desired.

s h e e r
c a n o p y

◆

Late afternoon and early evening—often the most pleasant and relaxing hours of a summer's day—can be ruined by the insects that come out to enjoy the balmy hours. A portable canopy, suspended from a rope or branch, is an excellent solution when flies and mosquitoes are troublesome.

As it made sense to be able to use the canopy indoors as well, I designed the shape to fit over a standard single bed, which gave me plenty of fabric to fit over an outdoor summer bed or reclining chair. The canopy is made from four pieces of delicate white cotton voile: a single panel that hangs behind the bed, a long rectangular panel that runs diagonally from the point of suspension to the floor, and two triangular side panels. The net is hung from a band of looped tabs the width of the back panel.

b e a c h
a w n i n g

◆

An all-day outing in full sunshine on the beach can
benefit from a good source of shade. Unlike a standard sun umbrella, this awning can accommodate a
family and all the trappings of an outing. The rectangular shape marks out your territory for the day and
provides a camp—somewhere to unload, spread out
a picnic, take a nap, read a book, and, for the children, somewhere to play out of the sun.

The design and construction could not be easier
—lengths of fabric have been machine stitched to
make up the size and grommets have been punched
into the four corners. The guy ropes are threaded
through the grommets and lashed to long bamboo
poles which are easily fixed into the sand. On a riverbank or in the woods, set aside the poles and simply
fix the ropes hammock-wise to four sturdy branches.

windbreak

◆

The times I have been lured outside by a bright sky only to find a cool breeze actively taking the heat out of the day are too numerous to mention. This is especially true on the beach, where sea breezes can quickly dampen a swimmer's enthusiasm! An old-fashioned windbreak is just the answer—it excludes the interloper and enjoyment resumes.

The windbreak can be made up of as many panels as you wish; usually there are three or four panels, sewn together with a long pocket between each panel for the supporting poles. Choose strong but lightweight fabrics. So they can withstand wear and tear, double-stitch seams with a heavy-duty sewing thread. I have avoided the obvious beachside deck chair and awning stripes and chosen solid blues and greens and finished the top edge with a decorative row of large silver grommets.

▶ 27

R

elax, put your feet up is one of the under-lying principles of outdoor living. This chapter looks at four simple means of doing just that (in comfort): the hammock, deck chair, floor cushion, and beach mat.

For comfort, use fabric that is soft and pleasing to the touch. For instance, replace the fabric on your deck chair with a prewashed canvas, cotton duck, or even linen. Lighter-weight cotton fabrics such as poplin and madras can also be used if lined. Do not use nylon fabric substitutes. Although they are available for this specific use and won't deteriorate if left out in the rain, they are hot and sticky to sit on, especially with bare skin, and will make a hot summer's day even hotter. This advice holds true for all of the projects. You need to feel comfortable in order to relax, which is why a wooden garden recliner, although attractive to the eye, gets short shrift when competing with anything like a hammock or deck chair with foot rest and canopy.

The four projects in this chapter can be made very economically in terms of both time and money, so the items do not have to be dragged in at first sight of inclement weather for fear of damage. They can be replaced easily. Re-covering a deck chair with canvas can be done for less than

twenty dollars. Be on the lookout for old deck chairs to refurbish. Often, old frames have more interesting lines than new ones, and, if you are really lucky, you might even find one with a foot rest and canopy. I picked up the chair on page 35 for six dollars, removed the nylon decking, stripped away the pale blue paint to reveal the natural color of the pine wood, and re-covered it with new canvas. The process took less than three hours.

LOUNGING

h a m m o c k

◆

A hammock strung between two leafy trees is the epitome of relaxation in the outdoors. It has so many happy and romantic associations, from the Mediterranean siesta to the castaway on a desert island. It truly does represent the easy life. Everyone is happy to idle away some time in the embrace of a hammock and be transported by the breeze, the hum of bees, and the perfume of the trees to their own desert island. A hammock is easy to make—it is simply a length of wood with a dozen holes drilled into it at regular intervals and some sturdy rope threaded through grommets in a length of strong fabric—with the color and pattern to your own taste. To make the hammock clews, you can use either natural or synthetic strings. Natural strings are more attractive, softer, and easier to work with. Synthetic strings, on the other hand, are stronger and won't disintegrate when left outdoors.

▶ 31

deck chair

◆

No summer is complete without at least one comedy routine of assembling a deck chair, and I suspect that we have all enjoyed a laugh at somebody else's expense as they frantically fashioned each new and fantastic shape. The practicality and comfort of deck chairs makes them well worth the occasional assembly hiccup. They fold flat and are wonderfully easy to store over the winter months, and their simple and robust design guarantees a long life. Unless subject to long bouts of wind and rain, a quality deck chair will last a long time. The only aspect that requires maintenance is the canvas, which may need replacing after two or three seasons, if only for cosmetic reasons. The decking is easily replaced and requires no more than a handful of tacks and a length of canvas, which you can buy in ready-cut deck-chair lengths from most good fabric suppliers.

LOUNGING

beach mat
and bag

◆

This neat double act is a must for all those sun wor-shipers who detest the thought of lugging furniture across the dunes, but who also want more comfort than a towel can provide. The beach mat is simply a 1- to 2-inch-thick piece of super-light foam covered with a removable sleeve. For portability, it rolls up easily to fit into a matching duffel bag (and makes for a very com-fortable head rest). For the sleeve, choose a soft cotton fabric that is comfortable to the skin and washes well at high temperatures. I chose seersucker, which comes in a good selection of bright and cheerful colors; other suitable fabrics are percale, madras, and chambray.

▶ 37

To give a maritime touch to the ensemble, use a thick, all-cotton cord for the drawstring. Drawn tight, it makes an attractive and decorative collar. Add a pocket to the outside of the bag to store your sunblock and other small personal items.

floor
cushion

◆

Cushions are an attractive component of comfort,
and the larger they are, the more inviting they
become. An oversized cushion on a blanket under a
shady tree is an ideal spot to escape to with a good
book. By its nature, a floor cushion should be
designed for a fair amount of wear and tear without
forsaking appearance. This "window" design cushion
is made using a sky blue linen-and-cotton blend with
a zipper at the bottom for easy maintenance. It is simply decorated with two squares of fabric in contrasting
colored applied with a chunky-look blanket stitch.

LOUNGING

accessories

A ccessories are those decorative items that we can do without but are better off for having—the icing on the cake, as it were. There are so many possible projects that could have been included in this chapter; birdhouses, bird feeders, planters, small furniture, a weather vane, and water fountain are just some ideas that were considered. The four I finally chose sum up the elements that constitute simple style; namely, function and simplicity of design, materials, and construction. Added to that, the design must be attractive and have a contemporary appeal. I also wanted projects that required no other skills than being able to follow a simple set of instruc-

tions. The lavender window box— is easy to make from materials that or have ready access to, and if you substitute them with another type The burlap tote bag is another project materials; although burlap can be pur- obtained as sacking when buying of pebbled paving stones always first-time visitors: "How wonderful;

an innovative recycling project— most of us either have in our garden don't have lavender stalks you can of aromatic semi-hardwood plant. that could make use of recycled chased off the bolt, it can also be animal feeds. The sight of a path generates the same response from I want to make some." Made of

such a humble everyday work material, these decorated concrete slabs seem to liberate the artist in all of us. The final project in this chapter is making container candles. They are an attractive, easy-to-make alternative to standard outdoor lighting and can be made in many variations. You can fill jam or tomato sauce jars, drinking glasses, and vases; you can use frosted glass and colored glass. Apart from glass there are pottery and ceramic containers as well as metal and heavy-duty plastics. Besides the obvious romance candlelight offers, container candles are an effective nontoxic insect deterrent that can be perfumed with your favorite scents.

▶ 45

ACCESSORIES

lavender
flower box

◆

Each year at the end of summer when I trim back the lavender, I begin thinking about what I can do with all the stalks. I've made the obvious—sachets, potpourri—and I've hung bunches up to dry, but that only uses a fraction of the harvest. I longed for something truly resourceful that would make good use of what would otherwise be added to the garden compost. I came up with an idea for an aromatic window box, woven from lavender cuttings, which would last through the winter months as a reminder of summer. Using an existing window box as a base, I ran garden wire around it to make a mesh through which to weave the lavender. When I had built up a thick layer of stalks, I simply slid the base out, leaving a freestanding container that I lined with heavy-duty black polyethylene before planting. This principle can be used to make boxes with other woody-stemmed herbs.

garden
candles

◆

Warm summer evenings beckon people outdoors for meals, conversation, or just simply to watch the stars. But some form of lighting is necessary. Evening is a romantic and peaceful time, and the light we use should reflect its softness. There are any number of lighting fixtures available to us today, from electric garden lights to small pin lights, but the most beautiful and evocative without question are candles. Container candles are easy to make, and the selection of shape and size is as wide as the variety of containers. The collection on the page opposite includes an assortment of glassware found in the kitchen—drinking glasses, jam jars, and a large vase. By adding a drop of fragrance to the wax you can keep the insects at bay, ensuring a truly peaceful evening.

Small canvas bags filled with wet sand and a night light make wonderful low-lying garden lights. Here they line the stone wall leading to the garden gate— perfect for outdoor parties.

burlap
tote bag

◆

I have made a concerted effort to avoid using the plastic carrier bags that have so invaded our lives. They have come to represent our buy-and-throw-away consumerism that is leaving a legacy of mountains and mountains of nondisposable plastic matter. I've made several of these easy-to-make tote bags using three of the most durable materials—burlap, ticking, and webbing. These old-time, workaday materials are sturdy and make a stylish but practical team. Lined with 100-percent cotton ticking, the bag is a suitable shopping tote and an all-purpose carrier for garden cuttings and produce. Hung up in the shed, unlined versions make excellent storage for bulbs, small tools, gardening paraphernalia, or dry pet foods.

pebble paving
stones

◆

Most of us are collectors, and we all seem to have a need to bring our experiences home in some tangible form. Who can refrain from pocketing occasional souvenir shells or colored beach glass, driftwood or smooth round pebbles. Over the years the collection grows until one day you are driven to ask yourself what to do with it all. Artist Wendy Wilbrahem knows exactly what do with the pebbles she collects—she integrates them into unusual pebble mosaics.

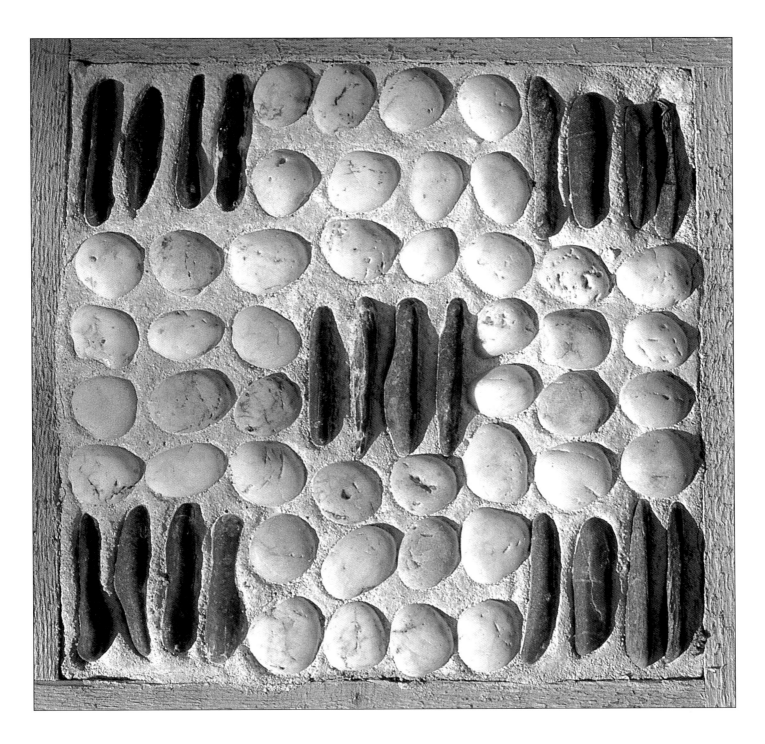

ACCESSORIES

Simplicity of material, design, and construction sums up simple style, and I felt the pebble paving stones project was perfect for this book. Wendy has designed a set of paving squares with a wandering floral motif that can be joined up in a linear fashion or into larger squares. Work out your design with just the pebbles on a square of paper before committing yourself to mixing the cement.

On the previous page is an example of a simple geometric design. The method of construction remains the same for whatever design you choose.

eating

E

ating *al fresco* is one of the great pleasures of life, whether it be a family barbecue on the patio, a party, a picnic, or a formal tea in the garden. It is a social activity that gives the occasion its vital ingredient—fun. At your next barbecue, stand back and observe for a moment—you will probably find everyone involved in the preparation—there's someone watching the barbecue, another cutting the bread, someone pouring drinks while others prepare salad or clean strawberries. And it is a very relaxed occasion, full of chatter.

A picnic basket of fairly average contents holds more excitement and

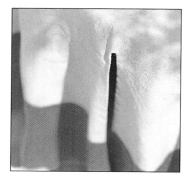

enjoyment than the same items served at the kitchen table. It is the ambience and the occasion that enhance the taste and look of food. The outdoors encourages people to relax—children and adults are free from the anxiety of spilling, and, in truth, fewer accidents seem to happen outdoors. And if the rogue glass of wine should fall, the outdoors takes it in stride by simply absorbing the incident, unlike a carpet, which would demand immediate, panicky attention.

Eating outdoors encourages simpler menus. The ferrying of hot food outside is not very practical, so dishes are adapted. We settle for more salads, fresh bread, barbecue-grilled meats and vegetables, cheese platters and fruit; in fact, an altogether healthy diet. It also means that the cook spends less time preparing and cooking meals and spends more time with the family or guests.

Table linens for the outdoors should be simple in design to maintain and reflect the casual mood of outdoor living. The four projects in this chapter cover all possible outdoor meals—simple placemats for a casual tea, linen tablerunners for a garden party, a colorful patchwork blanket for a picnic, and a two-toned tablecloth for a more formal occasion.

EATING

beaded tablerunners

◆

These long, beaded runners are ideal for dressing up a large buffet table and can be made using any fabric. I chose a raw linen so that the colors of the food and the bright ceramicware would look most inviting to the guests. Find a color and texture that look good with your china; try to avoid fussy florals, which will draw attention away from the food.

To add interest and detail, the hems are finished with neat miters that are brought to the right side of the fabric. To emphasize the pendant effect of the runners, I have dangled small handcarved wooden beads from the short sides. The beads are strung on linen threads of varying lengths drawn from a remnant of the same fabric, then knotted into the hem. Select beads that closely match your chosen fabric. There is such a large variety of beads available from various retail outlets that you should have no problem finding a perfect match.

buttoned
placemats

◆

These stripe-on-stripe placemats are simply construct-
ed from two rectangles of fabric—the smaller placed
on the larger and secured with four dainty shell buttons at each corner—so easy to make that a full set
can be machine-sewn in an afternoon. Using fabric of
the same design, make a set of placemats in different-
colors—one for each member of the family—and pair
them with plain-colored napkins. The secret to coordi-
nating many different colors is to make sure that all
are the same value.

The design is pleasant and can be comfortably
used for a summer's lunch or as settings for a casual
evening meal.

t w o - c o l o r
t a b l e c l o t h

◆

Bedecked in the bright warm colors of the Mediterranean, this tablecloth is suitable for any meal time, and can be dressed up or down to suit any occasion. With such lively colors for the background, choose your china with care, as liveliness on all sides makes for a very confused table. I chose rich brown Provençal earthenware to complement my two favorite colors, through this tablecloth will be equally effective in any number of colors. My first thought was to choose a soft teal blue offset with a delicate sea green, then the combination of musk pink and raspberry occupied my attention. Both ideas were abandoned when I envisioned the cloth with my china. For comfort when seated around the table, and to avoid the familiar tangle of guest and cloth, I designed it with slits that start at floor level and end almost at the table top.

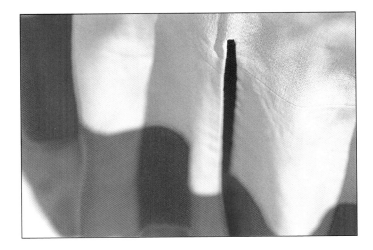

patchwork
picnic blanket

◆

Large, effervescent pink and orange rectangles surrounded by a bright lime green border are the elements that make up this eye-catching picnic blanket. The simple design allows you to make it in any combination of colors. You may prefer a less stimulating palette or you may want to introduce some patterned fabrics such as checks and ginghams to offset solid colors; such combinations will work just as effectively and lend a more rustic appeal. Large scale, brightly colored florals are another alternative for this design. This blanket is a great project for any beginner—the shapes are big and easy to handle, requiring only straight line seams, and the embellishment is a simple running stitch—an instant success!

66 ◀

▶ 69

M̲ake light work of your outdoor seating. Not all garden furniture can be left out of doors throughout the year: Wooden chairs can be treated with preserving oils and varnish finishes and metal furniture can be painted or sealed, but furniture incorporating fabrics will perish. It can withstand occasional showers but is best put away during the winter months. Bearing in mind your storage facilities, choose

chairs that are lightweight and can
Having a designated storage area
away quickly and easily if inclement
    The chairs in this chapter will
dining chairs, so they must provide
support—certainly enough to last
choosing your chairs, test them for
height of the table that they will be
chosen to dress up chairs that most

be folded or stacked conveniently.
also means that they can be put
weather persists.
most probably function as outdoor
a reasonable level of comfort and
through an entire meal. So when
comfort and take into account the
used with. For the projects, I have
people already have—the ubiquitous

director's chair, the common slatted garden chair, and the all-purpose folding picnic stool, which, although is not a first choice for a lengthy dinner, is an invaluable standby when extra seating is needed.
    Avoid polyester and synthetic fabrics for seating, as they are hot and sticky. You can pick up deck chair canvas, artist's canvas, and cotton duck very cheaply at art supply stores.

SEATING

envelope cushion covers

It is hard to believe that a sewing project could be so easy. Two linen tea towels and five buttons make up the materials list for this extremely stylish and practical cushion cover. There are many wonderful tea towels available, some patterned with checks or open grids, others with checkerboard designs or stripes. Conveniently, most are the exact width of a standard cushion pad. This means that you can utilize many of the woven border and trimming patterns in your cushion cover design. The only sewing required is stitching two cloths together to give sufficient length to wrap a cushion front and back with a generous flap and adding buttonholes.

   The cover is sealed on the sides with two small buttons. For extra strength, you may want to sew a small length of bias tape to the sides before making the buttonholes.

cushioned chair back
& seat covers

◆

Although attractive to look at, wooden garden chairs don't always provide the level of comfort that we would like, so that getting through a meal can be hard work. You can add cushion pads to the seats, but they slide off unless fastened to the chair; in any case, that solution still leaves your back resting against the hard wooden slats. The chair back cover is a simple design consisting of two rectangles of fabric with slightly tapered ends sandwiching a thick layer of wadding. The cover folds over the back and front of the chair back and is secured by tie fasteners on either side of the chair. Easy to remove for washing and storage, this cover idea is simple to make and an effective way to soften an "obdurate" chair.

76 ◀

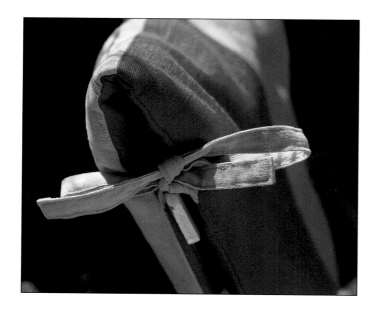

S E A T I N G

director's chair cover

◆

Director's chairs provide a cheap and comfortable form of seating for outdoors. Lightweight and fold-away, they are ideal portable furniture.

The frames, usually made of wood with metal bracing, are quite sturdy and will last several seasons. The canvas back and seat, on the other hand, will probably need replacing, if only for cosmetic reasons. There are several types of director's chairs and the instructions given can be adapted to fit any type. Choose fabric colors and patterns that coordinate with other items of garden furniture. For easy maintenance, use only quality cotton fabrics that can be washed at high temperatures. I chose a colorful madras cotton for the chair cover shown opposite, while for the cover of the formal outdoor dining chair on page 68, I chose a crisp, white cotton-and-linen blend.

folding
picnic stool

◆

Obviously ideal for away-from-home activities such as picnics and sporting events, where weight and portability are of concern, folding stools are also invaluable when additional seating is needed for a garden party. Although most guests are happy to stand, many will welcome a short respite off their feet, especially when trying to negotiate food, drink, and conversation at the same time.

The canvas seat comprises a small rectangle of fabric with channels on either side, which slide onto the metal frame. These stools are so simple to make, you can make a new set for any special occasion and paint the metal frame to match. To offset the bright pink and orange seating and lend a contemporary look, I painted the frames with silver to mimic a galvanized silver finish.

putting it together

To make *Simple Outdoor Style* accessible to all readers, projects have been designed that employ the simplest and most obvious methods of construction. The non-sewing projects require a sprinkling of common sense and the ability to follow some basic instructions. The sewing projects require no special skill beyond being able to sew a straight seam on a sewing machine. Although all items can be sewn by hand, for strength and durability and for ease of sewing, machine sewing is advisable.

The success of the projects depends largely on your choice of materials, the colors, and the finish. Take time in choosing your materials and always buy what pleases you; try not to compromise because you'll only be dissatisfied with it further on down the line and then abandon it. Choose the best quality materials available. Although initially more expensive, they will handle and wear better and stand the test of time.

All the projects have been made using natural products: 100-percent cotton or linen fabrics, sisal rope and bamboo for the beach awning, cotton rope for the hammock clews, burlap for the tote bag. Natural products are usually easier to handle and often wear better. The exception is rope: nylon rope is stronger and will not disintegrate.

The equipment needed for making any of the projects is basic and can be found in most households: sewing machine, scissors, and pins for the sewing projects; pliers and garden wire for the lavender box; saucepan and scales for the candles; and bucket and spade for the pebble paving stones. For the projects requiring grommets, such as the hammock, beach awning, and windbreak, grommet kits can be found at fabric and notions stores. If, however, you are using a particularly heavy fabric for any of these projects, take a sample swatch with you to the store to make certain that the kits available are suitable for your choice of fabric. If not, then have the grommets punched in professionally. Most blind-making companies, awning manufacturers, and upholsterers can provide this service.

parasol changing tent

◆

To adapt the panels to fit your parasol, measure the width of each parasol section and the height from the shade to the ground.

MATERIALS
◆ *Pre-purchased octagonal-shape parasol*
◆ *12yd/11m fabric to match*
◆ *Curtain rings – 40*
◆ *Sewing kit*

1 Cut eight 33 x 85in/84 x 216cm panels.

2 Press a ¼in/0.75cm seam all around. Turn in another 1¼in/3cm and press.

3 Miter the corners: unfold the seams and turn in the corners. Clip the diagonal, leaving a small seam allowance. Turn in the seam. Refold the edges.

4 Press, then hand stitch the miter.

5 To make the ties, cut 40 2 x 22in/5 x 56cm strips. Turn in ½in/1.5cm at each short end. Press. Fold each strip in half lengthways. Press. Open out the fold. Turn in the raw edges to the center fold. Refold, then stitch across each short end and down the long edge. *(see picture next column)*

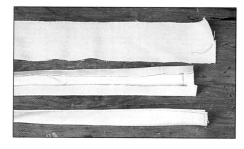

6 Fold the tie in half and pin to the top right-hand corner of the wrong side of the panel. Add a second tie to the top center. To the top left-hand side stitch a curtain ring. Stitch three ties at even intervals to the left-hand side of the panel. Stitch three curtain rings to correspond on the right-hand side.

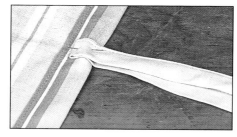

7 Add rings to correspond with the ties.

beach awning

◆

This awning can be made to any size and height and almost any shape. Keep the poles and awning in proportion. Choose a sturdy all-cotton fabric or canvas that can withstand substantial wear and tear.

MATERIALS
◆ 3 1/2yd/3.2m strong cotton fabric
◆ Grommets
◆ Bamboo poles
◆ Rope
◆ Sewing kit

1 Cut the fabric in half across the width and sew the two halves together along the length.

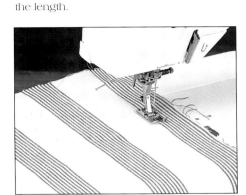

2 Turn under 2in/5cm at each edge and press. Turn under another 2in/5cm and press again.

3 Double topstitch along all edges.

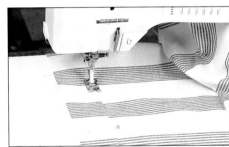

4 Following the manufacturer's instructions, insert a grommet in each corner.

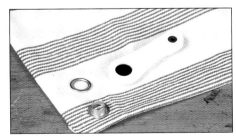

sheer canopy

◆

This canopy is made up of four sections: a rectangle for the back, two right-angle triangles for the sides, and one other rectangle for the front.

● Cut the largest pieces from the fabric first.

1 For the front panel, cut one length 129in/328cm.

2 At one short edge, for the bottom, turn in ¼in/0.75cm. Press. Turn in another 1½in/3.75cm. Press and stitch.

3 Turn in a double hem at each long side. Press and stitch.

4 For the back, cut one length 82in/208cm. Turn in a hem at the bottom edge. Turn in a double hem at each side.

5 Make a paper pattern for the triangular sides. The longest vertical side of the triangle is 82in/208cm long. The horizontal, representing the bottom edge of the canopy is 84in/214cm wide. Draw a diagonal joining the two points. (The diagram below illustrates the point where the second piece of fabric is joined to the width of the first piece.)

6 Cut and piece the shape from fabric. Where two pieces of fabric join, sew together with a fell seam so that no raw edges are visible.

7 Turn the pattern over for the opposite side.

8 At the bottom edge, turn in ¼in/0.75cm, press, then turn in another 1½in/3.75cm. Press and stitch. Turn in a double hem at each side.

9 One at a time, pin the diagonal edge of the side panels to the long edges of the front, right sides together.

10 Start at the top edge and stitch together to within 24in/61cm of the bottom edge.

11 Place the back and front right sides together, aligning top raw edges. Pin together.

12 Run a gathering thread through the top edge and pull up the threads to 40in/100cm wide.

MATERIALS

◆ *11yd/10m cotton voile 60in/152cm wide*

◆ *Sewing kit*

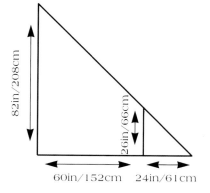

82in/208cm

26in/66cm

60in/152cm   24in/61cm

13 For the band to hold the tabs at the top of the net, cut two pieces of voile 4 x 41in/10 x 105cm.

14 Fold each in half lengthways, wrong sides together, and press.

15 Align the raw edge of one band with the gathered raw edges of the canopy at the front. Slide the band down so that it sits 1 1/2 in/3.75cm below the gathered raw edges. Pin. Add the second band to the same position at the back. Baste the raw edges in place.

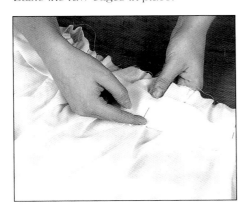

16 Stitch the top raw edge of the bands in place, stitching through all the layers at the same time.

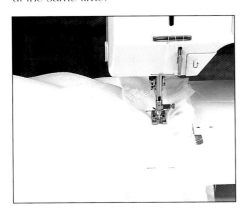

17 Trim the excess fabric away from the top of the canopy to reduce the bulk behind the waistband.

18 To make the tabs to hang the net, cut five pieces 2 1/2 x 6in/6.5 x 15cm.

19 Turn in the raw edges on each long edge and press.

20 Fold the tab in half lengthways, press, then stitch to hold. Fold in half across the width, press.

21 Position one tab at each end of the band, placing one raw edge at each side of the gathered raw edge. Pin.

22 Space the remaining tabs evenly across the band. Hold in place with a few basting stitches. Remove the pins.

23 Fold the band up over the raw edges of the tabs and the gathers and pin in place. Topstitch to hold.

24 Hold the canopy in place by sliding a length of cane through the tabs. The canopy should drape loosely over the sun lounger.

▶ 89

windbreak

◆

The windbreak can be made up of as many panels as you wish. If you choose a particularly heavy fabric, it is advisable to use a professional grommet punching service.

MATERIALS

- ◆ 1yd/1m of 54in/137cm wide navy
- ◆ 1yd/1m of 54in/137cm wide sky blue
- ◆ 1yd/1m of 54in/137cm wide pink
- ◆ 1yd/1m of 54in/137cm wide green
- ◆ 32 grommets 1½in/4cm in diameter
- ◆ 5 bamboo poles

1 Trim each panel to 48in/122cm wide.

2 At the top and bottom of each panel, turn under ½in/1.5cm. Press. Turn under another 2½in/6.5cm for the grommet band. Press. Machine topstitch in place. *(see picture next column)*

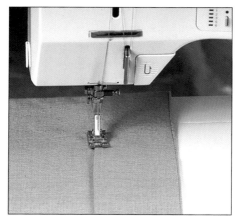

3 Arrange the panels according to your preferred color scheme. On alternate panels, at each side, turn under ½in/1.5cm to the wrong side. Press. On the remaining two panels, turn under ½in/1.5cm to the right side. Press.

4 Overlap the first panel with the second by 2in/5cm at one side, ensuring the overlap is sufficient to insert the poles and the raw edges are enclosed. Pin.

5 Double topstitch at each folded edge. Repeat to add the remaining panels.

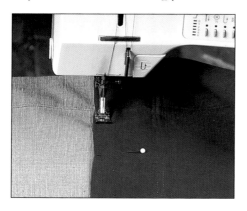

6 At the outside edges, turn in 1½in/ 4cm. Press and double topstitch to give a neat finish.

7 Insert the grommets at evenly spaced intervals according to the manufacturer's instructions, four at the top and four at the bottom of each panel.

8 Insert the bamboo poles to finish.

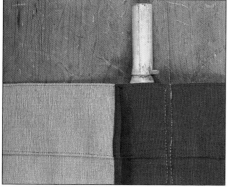

d e c k   c h a i r

◆

If you are replacing a canvas, measure up the old decking and cut the new canvas to that measurement. If you have found an old frame, roughly estimate 1¹/₂yd/1.3m for a standard chair x the width of the seat.

horizontal bar
second row of tacks

horizontal bar
first row of tacks

MATERIALS
- 1¹/₂yd/1.3m canvas
- Small round-headed tacks or nails
- Hammer
- Sandpaper

1 Remove the old canvas. Clean the frame by sanding lightly or scrubbing with warm water and mild detergent.

2 If you have stripped away any paint finish, preserve the wood by lightly rubbing in teak oil with a soft cloth.

3 At each short end, turn under 1in/ 2.5cm. Press and turn under another 1in/2.5cm and press again.

4 Using five or six tacks, fix one end of the canvas to the lower horizontal bar.

5 Wrap the canvas once around the bar to conceal the tacks.

6 Take the canvas over the top horizontal bar, bringing the end to the front of the bar but concealed below the canvas.

7 Spacing the tacks evenly, secure the canvas in place. This is a little awkward and you may find it helpful if you have another pair of hands to hold up the canvas while you hammer in the tacks.

hammock

◆

Use the instructions below to make a new hammock or adapt or renovate an old one.

MATERIALS

◆ *3yd/3m of yellow and green canvas 54in/137cm wide*

◆ *20yd/20m of ½in/1.5cm wide rope*

◆ *Wooden batten 1yd/1m long with twelve evenly spaced holes large enough to thread the rope through*

◆ *Two steel rings 2–3in/5–7.5cm in diameter*

◆ *26 grommets*

◆ *Sewing kit*

1 Square up the fabric. Turn in ¾in/2cm across the width for the top and bottom. Press. Turn in another 2in/5cm and press. Double topstitch in place.

2 Repeat step 1 for turning in the sides.

3 Find the center of the top and bottom seams and mark with a pin. This is the position of the center grommet.

4 Measure and mark with pins the position of six evenly spaced grommets to each side of the center pin.
(see picture next column)

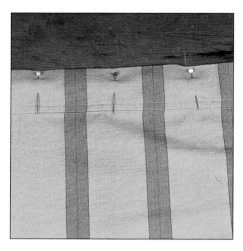

5 Insert the grommets following the manufacturer's instructions. (*see figs 1–4 below*)

Fig 1

Fig 2

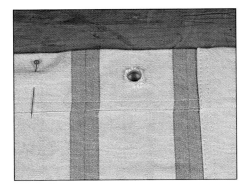

Fig 3

Fig 4

6 Thread a double thickness of rope through each side seam. Make a knotted loop at each end. (*see picture at bottom of column*)

7 With a third length of rope, leaving a long thread end, begin at the left-hand side of the wooden batten and thread through the loop, then through the first hole at the left-hand side of the batten working from bottom to top.

8 Thread the rope through the metal ring above the center of the batten, and then back through the second hole in the batten.

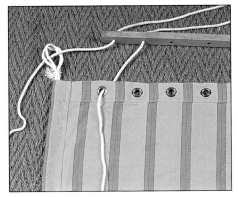

9 Thread the rope down through the first grommet.

10 Thread through the next two grommets, up through the batten to the ring and back. Repeat. (*see pic below*)

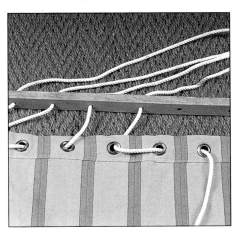

11 At the right-hand side thread the rope through the batten and knot the end around the loops at the end of the side seam. Repeat at the other end.

floor cushion

◆

Finished size: 26 x 26in/66 x 66cm

This cushion design can be adapted to fit any size cushion pad.

MATERIALS

◆ 1¾yd/1.6m blue
◆ 18 x 18in/46 x 46cm white
◆ One skein each blue and white wool
◆ 22in/55cm white zipper
◆ Sewing kit

1 Cut two blue squares 27½in/70cm for the cushion front and back.

2 For the appliqué decoration, cut one white square 17½ x 17½in/44.5 x 44.5cm. Cut one blue square 7½ x 7½in/19 x 19cm.

3 Press under ¾in/2cm around the raw edge of each appliqué square. Trim the diagonal at each corner to reduce the bulk. Center the small blue square on the white square. Pin, machine stitch close to the edge.
(see picture next column)

4 Decorate the edge with blanket stitch.

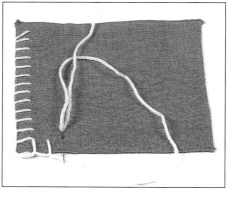

5 Repeat to stitch the white square to the cushion front.

6 To insert the zipper, pin and baste the cushion front and back right sides together along one edge. Measure and mark the centered zipper position. Machine-stitch the cushion front and back together at each side of the zipper position, taking a ¾in/2cm seam.
(see picture next column)

7 Press the seam open. On the seam, position the zipper right side down over the basted area. Pin. Using a zipper foot, stitch the zipper in position, without catching the teeth of the zipper.

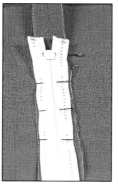

8 Open the zipper slightly. Stitch the cushion front to the cushion back using a ¾in/2cm seam and rounding the corners. Overcast the raw edges.

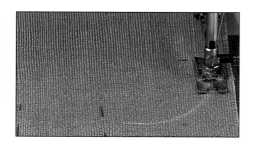

beach mat and bag

◆

BEACH BAG

Finished size: 13in/33cm diameter 29in/74cm long

Seersucker is an ideal choice for this beach-side ensemble. The bag is a drawstring tube that neatly stows the mat for carrying. Add a small pocket on the inside to house valuables.

MATERIALS

◆ *1yd/1m of 44in/112cm wide blue seersucker for the base and bag top*
◆ *44 x 30in/112 x 76cm green check seersucker for the bag body*
◆ *Green cord for the handle*
◆ *Paper for template*
◆ *Sewing kit*

1 Make a paper template of a 14in/35.75cm diameter circle for the bag base. Cut one from blue fabric. For the bag top, cut one piece 17 x 44in/44 x 112cm from blue.

2 Stitch the bag top to the green check, along the 44in/112cm edge. Press the seam open. Turn in a double hem at the 44in/112cm raw edge of the blue and baste.

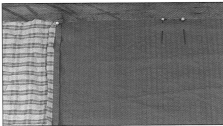

3 Fold and pin the fabric in half lengthways, right sides together. On the blue seam line, measure and mark points 6in and 7in/15cm and 18cm from the seam joining the green check. The 1in/3cm gap marks the point where the cord handle will be threaded through.

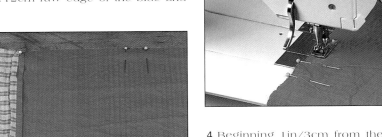

4 Beginning 1in/3cm from the basted double hem of the blue, stitch the side seam, reinforcing the stitching at each side of the 1in/3cm gap.

5 At the top of the tube, turn down 5in/12.75cm to the wrong side, so that the open seam at the top of the bag aligns with the gap in the side seam. Press and pin. Mark the channel for the cord handle.

6 Stitch the edge of the channel closest to the top of the bag, so that the stitching clears the channel. Reinforce the stitching at the top of the gap.

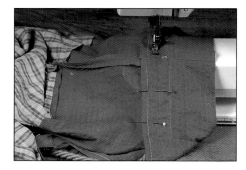

7 Place the cord close to the stitched line. Anchor in place, then stitch the fabric together, enclosing the cord in the channel.

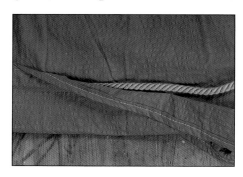

8 With right sides together, fit the bag base to the tube. Pin and stitch.

BEACH MAT COVER

Tailor-made to fit a length of foam, this simple idea can be adapted for any size and thickness of mat. The cover can be easily removed for washing.

MATERIALS
◆ Green-and-blue check seersucker – 4yd/4m
◆ Scraps of blue for the ties
◆ Foam – 70 x 32 x 1½in/1.8m x 80 x 3.5cm thick

● Use ½in/1.5cm seam allowances unless otherwise stated.

1 For the ties, cut four lengths 2 x 12in/5 x 30.5cm. Turn in ¼in /0.75cm seam at each short edge. Press. Turn in ¼in/0.75cm along each long edge. Press. Fold the tie in half lengthways, wrong sides together. Press. Machine topstitch around the folded edges.

2 For the mat top and bottom, cut two pieces of fabric the length and width of the foam plus seam allowances.

3 From the remainder, for the envelope-style flap, cut one piece the width of the mat plus seam allowances x 12in/ 30.5cm long.

4 For the sides, measure the thickness of the foam, and cut two pieces the length of the foam x the thickness, plus seam allowances. Cut two pieces the width of the foam x the thickness plus seam allowances.

5 Join a long length to each side of one short length. Press the seams open. Set aside the remaining short length.

6 Pin the length for the sides to the beachmat top, right sides together.

7 Align raw edges and begin stitching down one long edge. Stop stitching ½in/1.5cm from the corner. Lift the machine foot.

8 Fold the side strip up at 45° angle away from the quilt, then bring it back down to align with the next side.

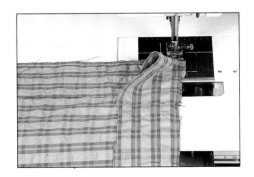

9 The movement will create a pleat at the corner, allowing sufficient fabric to create a miter.

10 Continue stitching around the three sides.

11 When you return to the top, turn in ½in/1.5cm across the raw edge and press.

12 Pin two ties 3in/7.5cm from each seam joining the side to the top. Stitch the turning. Set aside.

13 Turn in a small seam at each short end of the remaining side strip.

14 Center the strip along one short edge of the bottom panel of the beach mat. Stitch the two together. Set aside.

15 Turn in and stitch a seam allowance around three sides of the envelope flap, leaving one long edge free.

16 Align the raw edge of the envelope flap with that of the side strip at the short end of the bottom panel. Pin. *(see picture next column)*

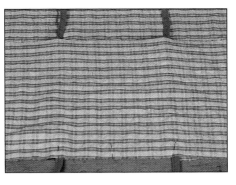

17 Between the bottom panel and the envelope flap, place the ties 3in/7.5cm from each raw edge. Stitch together.

18 With right sides together, pin the two halves of the beach mat together.

19 Machine stitch the two sides together. Turn right side out to finish and insert the foam mat.

20 If you choose, use the ties for decoration only and slipstitch the green check seersucker closed at the top edge.

garden candles

◆

Candle making has become such a popular activity that you should be able to find most of the necessary materials at your local art and craft stores. There are specialized candle making suppliers that offer mail order services.

MATERIALS

◆ *Candle making wax*
◆ *Beeswax*
◆ *Nylon wicks*
◆ *Sustainers*
◆ *Slugs (weight)*
◆ *Pencil (or thin rod will do)*
◆ *Thin knitting needle or similar*
◆ *Containers*
◆ *Old saucepans*
◆ *Pliers*

1 Collect all your materials together. Protect your work surfaces with newspaper.

2 Heat up your glass containers by standing them in a tray of warm water, then place in the oven at the lowest temperature setting. Leave until ready to fill with the melted wax. Ensure that the inside of the container does not get wet.

3 Melt the candle wax and beeswax slowly in a saucepan. Do not put the saucepan directly on the heat source. Use a double boiler or place the saucepan in a larger container, as shown.

4 Cut a length of wick the depth of your container plus approximately 2in/5cm extra for tying on the sustainer and slug and winding around the rod.

5 Attach a sustainer to one end of the wick and fix in place by crimping the neck with a pair of long-nosed pliers.

6 Thread on the slug so that it sits on top of the sustainer. The weight will help keep the wick in the correct position.

7 When the wax has melted, allow it to cool to approximately 158°F/70°C. Add any fragrances or insect repellents at this point and stir in gently.

8 Holding the wick so that it hangs just above the bottom of the container, pour the melted wax into the warm container.

9 Wind the end of the wick around a thin rod or pencil.

10 As the wax cools it shrinks in the middle, making a well. To prevent this from happening, prick the center every 10 minutes until set. After approximately an hour, top up with melted wax.

11 When the wax is hard, trim the wick.

burlap tote bag

◆

Finished size: 19 x 11in/48.25 x 28cm

This practical tote bag, made of burlap and ticking, will withstand the wear and tear of outdoor life.

MATERIALS
◆ *12in/30cm burlap*
◆ *12in/30cm green-and-white ticking*
◆ *1¾yd/1.6m bias tape for handles*
◆ *Sewing kit*

● Use ½in/1.5cm seams throughout.

1 Cut the ticking into two equal size pieces and square up the edges.

2 Square up the burlap length and overcast the raw edges to stop the threads from fraying.

3 With right sides together, align the 12in/30cm raw edge of ticking with one short edge of burlap. Stitch the two together. Repeat at the other end of the burlap. Press without distorting the burlap. (*see picture top of next column*)

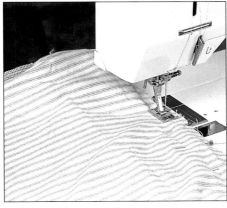

4 Refold the burlap in half across the width, right sides together and pin the side seams. Machine-stitch the seams, reinforcing the stitching across the seams joining the burlap to the ticking.

5 Turn the bag right side out. Press.

6 At the remaining raw edge of the ticking, turn in a small hem and press. On the right side of the fabric, stitch the folded edges of the ticking together to form the lining bag bottom.

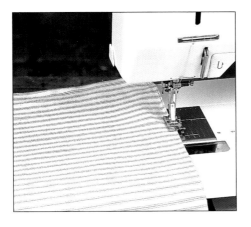

7 Push the lining into the burlap bag. Turn back 3in/7.5cm of ticking to show on the burlap side of the bag.

8 Cut the handle tape in half. Turn under the raw edges and press. Pin the handles in position and stitch through all the fabric layers, reinforcing the tape ends with a square of stitching.

lavender flower box

◆

This is a seasonal project that can be replaced each year. Try other aromatic cuttings such as sage, thyme, rosemary, and marjoram. If you do not have enough of one variety, use different stems in combination.

MATERIALS
- ◆ *A plastic or terracotta window box*
- ◆ *Garden wire*
- ◆ *Pliers*
- ◆ *Large quantity of fresh lavender*
- ◆ *Florists' scissors*
- ◆ *Heavy-duty polyethylene for the flower box liner*

1 Wind lengths of garden wire in parallel horizontal bands around your base window box. Secure each length by twisting the ends around each other. Do not make the bands too tight or you will find it impossible to thread the lavender.
(see picture next column)

2 Repeat to make vertical bands by centering each length under the base of the window box and weaving the remaining sections through the horizontal bands to make a grid.

3 Using the longest stalks, thread the lavender vertically through the grid all around the box.
(see picture next column)

4 Repeat, weaving the stalks horizontally until you have a close weave.

5 Trim the vertical stalks flush with the top edge of the box.

6 Use the trimmed stalks to fill any gaps.

7 Gently ease the woven lavender away from the base.

8 Line with heavy-duty plastic and make some drainage holes in the base. Put the lavender box in position in your garden before filling with potting compost and planting.

pebble paving stones

◆

Finished size: 15 x 15in/38 x 38cm

From the picture below you can see how easy it is to create a paving stone design. Use rubber gloves when handling cement.

MATERIALS

- ◆ *Length of wood 1in/2.5cm thick and long enough to make a frame for four sides of the tile*
- ◆ *A length of wood to use as a straight edge*
- ◆ *Hammer and nails*
- ◆ *Selection of pebbles*
- ◆ *Sand and cement*

1 Cut four lengths of wood for the frame and fix the pieces together.

2 On a flat surface, arrange the pebbles as required in the base of the frame. Remove the pebbles.

3 Following the manufacturer's instructions, make up a mix of concrete. Pour into the frame.

4 Drag a length of wood across the surface of the wet concrete until it is flat. Remove any excess, or fill in any dips in the surface and level again in the same way.

5 Add the pebbles to the surface in the required arrangement. Allow the concrete to dry.

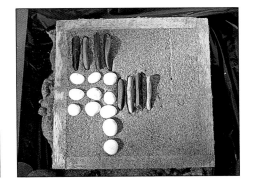

6 Tap the wooden frame to release the paving stone.

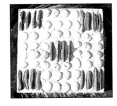

buttoned placemats

◆

Finished size: 17 x 13in/43.25 x 33cm

These easy-to-make pastel-colored mats are finished with attractive shell buttons and make a beautiful summer table setting.

MATERIALS

◆ *18 x 14in/46 x 36cm narrow blue stripe*
◆ *11½ x 9in/30 x 23cm wide blue stripe*
◆ *4 shell buttons*
◆ *Sewing kit*

1 Turn in and press ¼in/0.75cm along each raw edge of the narrow blue stripe fabric. Turn in another ¼in/0.75cm and press. Machine-stitch to hold.

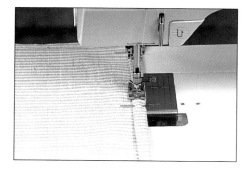

2 Repeat with the wide blue stripe decorative rectangle.

3 Center the decorative rectangle on the placemat. Pin.

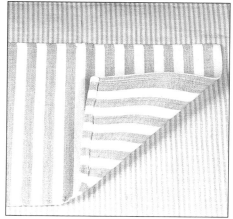

4 Position a button at each corner and handstitch in place through all the layers. Remove the pins.

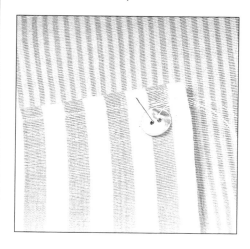

beaded tablerunners

◆

Finished size: 20 x 59½in/50.75 x 151.25cm

On this simple pair of runners I have made a feature of the hem, bringing the turning to the right side.

MATERIALS

To make one runner:
- ◆ *22½ x 62in/57 x 157.5cm natural-color linen*
- ◆ *A selection of carved wooden beads*
- ◆ *Linen thread*
- ◆ *Sewing kit*

1 Turn in ¼in/0.75cm all around the linen edge. Press. Turn in another 1in/2.5cm. Press. Unfold the turnings.

2 Turn in each corner. Clip the fabric at a diagonal to reduce the bulk, leaving a small seam allowance.
(see picture next column)

3 On a remnant of fabric, fray the threads and pull away several lengths on which to thread the beads.

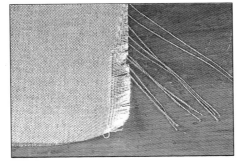

4 Knot one bead onto the end of a 6in/15cm length of thread.

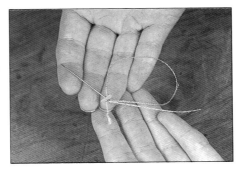

5 String several beads and make a knot in the thread to hold them in place. To leave a gap, make a large knot and continue threading beads.

6 Stitch the lengths of beaded thread at equal intervals to the second foldline and make a knot so that the thread end will be caught in the seam.

7 Refold the tablerunner seams and hand stitch the miter.

8 Machine-stitch the seam in place ¾in/2cm from the folded edge.

two-color tablecloth

◆

Adapt the measurements to fit your own round table

A stylish, lined circular tablecloth with four slits from the floor to the table top.

MATERIALS

- ◆ *6yd/5.5m main color*
- ◆ *2¹/8yd/2m contrasting color*
- ◆ *5¹/2yd/5m lining*
- ◆ *Paper to make a pattern*
- ◆ *Chalk marker*
- ◆ *Sewing kit*

1 Cut the main color in half across the width. Join the pieces together along one long edge. Press the seam open. *(see picture next page, column 1)*

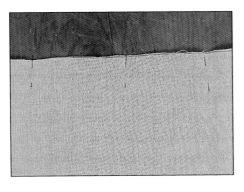

2 Fold the fabric into quarters, right sides together.

3 Measure the diameter of the table, add on twice the height of the tablecloth plus 4in/10cm for seams.

4 Make a paper pattern for a quarter of the tablecloth. Round one corner.

5 For the pattern for the contrasting band, draw another arc inside the first, 9in/22cm away.

6 Pin the main color pattern to the fabric and carefully cut out the circle.

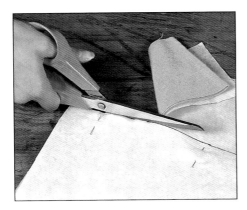

7 The contrasting border is cut on the bias and is pieced together.

8 Cut the pattern for the contrasting band into sections small enough to fit the width of your fabric. It may help to cut more than one pattern from paper.

9 Place the pattern at one end of the fabric. Using a fabric marker, lightly draw around the pattern piece.

10 Fill the fabric with the required number of sections, remembering to leave a seam allowance all around each for joining the sections together.

11 Cut out each piece, adding the seam allowance by eye as you cut.

12 Piece the sections of contrasting fabric together until you have a complete circle for the hem.

13 Press the seams out flat. Try the fit of the contrasting band and adapt the seams where necessary.

14 Turn in a seam allowance around the raw edge of the main color. Pin to the contrasting band. Topstitch in place.

15 Turn in a seam allowance around the raw edge of the contrasting band. Press.

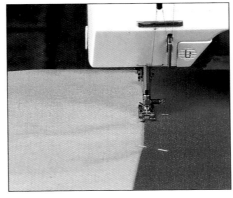

16 Place the cloth over the table and, with a chalk marker and a straight edge, mark the position of the slits.

17 Spread the cloth on a flat surface and cut the slits following the marked lines.

18 Turn the raw edges a scant $1/8$in/0.5cm to the wrong side of the cloth and fingerpress, then slipstitch in place.

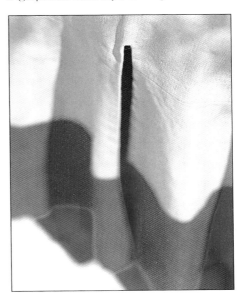

19 If your table is adapted to take an umbrella, cut a small circle in the center of the tablecloth large enough to accommodate the umbrella pole. Turn under a small seam and press.

20 Cut and piece the lining to fit the tablecloth.

21 Turn in a small seam at the raw edges at the center of the lining and outer edges. Pin the lining to the cloth.

22 Slipstitch the lining in place.

patchwork picnic blanket

◆

Finished size: 61 x 52in/155 x 132cm

Patchwork at its simplest, this is a fast and easy project for you to make using cotton sheeting.

MATERIALS
- ◆ *2yd/2m lime green*
- ◆ *1yd/1m orange*
- ◆ *1yd/1m pink*
- ◆ *1¾yd /1.6m of 54in/137cm wide heavyweight cotton fabric for backing*
- ◆ *Thick navy thread*
- ◆ *Sewing kit*
- ◆ *Pencil and ruler*

1 Cut six pink and six orange rectangles 9½ x 15½in/24 x 39.5cm—twelve in total.

2 For the border, cut two lime green strips 65 x 10½in/165 x 26.75cm and two borders 56 x 10½in/142.25 x 26.75cm.

3 On a clean, flat surface, arrange the pink and orange rectangles, four wide and three deep, alternating the colors throughout.

4 Using ¼in/0.75cm seam allowance, stitch the rectangles into the three rows.

5 Stitch the three rows together.

6 Along one long edge of each border, find and mark with a pin the center-point. Find the center of each side of the cloth and match the two points. With right sides together, pin each border to the cloth, allowing the excess to overlap at each edge.

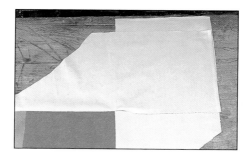

7 Stitch each border in place. Begin stitching ¼in/0.75cm from the raw edge of the cloth.

8 To miter the corners, press under the ¼in/0.75cm seam allowance on the inside raw edge of each border.

9 Fold the cloth diagonally at each corner and, with a pencil and ruler, draw a diagonal line at an accurate 45° angle. Baste along the line, then open out the cloth and check that the miter lies flat. Adjust as necessary.

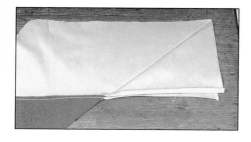

10 Machine stitch the miter. Trim away the excess border.

11 The border is 8in/20cm wide. Turn in the excess and press. Fold in a diagonal at each corner across the point where the two pressed lines cross. Trim away the corners, leaving a small seam. Refold the seams and stitch the miter.

12 With navy thread, sew the running stitch decoration. Cut the backing ½in/1.5cm smaller than the cloth. Turn in a seam and press. Slipstitch the backing in place.

envelope cushion covers

◆

Finished size: 18 x 19¼in/46 x 49cm

The envelope cushion cover is a novel and extremely economical way of using 100-percent linen tea towels.

MATERIALS

- ◆ *Two purchased tea towels*
- ◆ *2¾yd/2.5m of 1¼in/3cm-wide bias tape for the button band*
- ◆ *Five buttons ¾in/2cm diameter*
- ◆ *Sewing kit*

● Use ¼in/0.75cm seam throughout.

1 Turn in a hem around each edge of the tea towels, press and machine stitch in place.

2 Stitch two towels together at one short edge. Press the seam open.

3 Cut the button-band tape in half. Machine-stitch the tape along the long edges of the wrong side of the cushion so that it covers the turned-in edge. Trim away any excess.

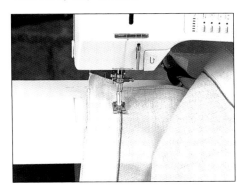

4 At one short end, turn in 2in/5cm and press. Stitch in place close to the folded-down edge.

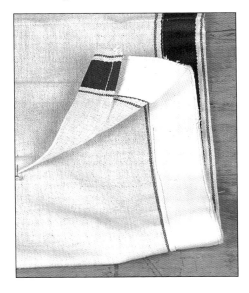

5 Make three evenly spaced buttonholes along this edge.

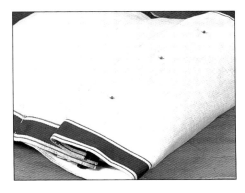

6 At the opposite short edge, turn down 3in/7.5cm. Press and stitch. Sew on three buttons to correspond with the buttonholes.

7 Halfway down the right- and left-hand side of the button band, make one buttonhole.

8 Stitch on two buttons to correspond with the buttonholes.

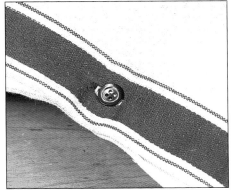

director's chair cover

◆

Follow the directions below to make a cover for your director's chair. The directions can be adapted to suit other chair variations.

MATERIALS

◆ *Pink, orange, and purple madras check*

◆ *16 grommets 1in/2.5cm in diameter*

◆ *Large sheets of paper*

◆ *Sewing kit*

1 Measure the height and width of the front of the chair back. Add on the thickness of the chair sides and top (A).

2 Measure the depth and width of the seat (B). Add 4¹/₂in/12cm to the depth.

3 Measure the width and drop from the top of the chair arm to the seat (C);
● the width of the arm and the length from the back to the chair D); and

● the width and drop from the top of the arm to the floor (E). To the width of E add 5in/13cm. Double the fabric quantity for C, D, and E—one set for each side.

4 Measure the width of the chair and the drop from the front of the seat to the floor (F), then measure the back of the chair from the top to the floor (G). To the width of F and G add 5in/13cm.

5 To all your measurements add a 1/2in/1.5cm seam all around, except for the hem edges of E, F, and G, to which you should add a 4in/10cm hem.

6 With the patterns, make a mock-up to ensure a good fit without straining the seams.

7 Cut each pattern from fabric.

8 Cut eight ties 14 x 3 1/4in/35 x 8cm.

9 Center the base of A to the back of B. Make a pleat 2 1/4in/6cm deep in B, parallel to A. Sew the pleat, then keep the pleat free during assembly.

10 Sew D to the top and front edge of C. Stitch to within a seam allowance width of the corner of C. Lift the presser foot. Rotate, then realign D and stitch the second side in place.

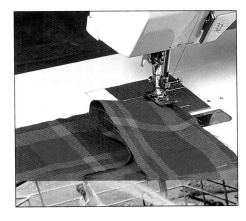

11 Try the fit over the arm. Make another in reverse.

12 Stitch the lower edge of C to B. Sew the vertical of C to the cut-out edge of A. Sew the end of D to the top of the cut-out (it does not complete the cut-out). Repeat at both sides.

13 Press in a double 1 1/4in/3cm seam at both sides of E, F, and G. Unfold the hems and keep clear of the stitching. Sew the top of E across the cut-out on A, along D and down the front edge of D. Repeat on the other arm. Center F to

B and sew, continuing across the lower ends of D.

14 Center the top of G to A and sew. With the hem edges of E and G level, sew G to E and A at the sides from a point level with seam B–F on the front upwards.

15 To make the fabric fit at the top of the chair, on each side seam to align with the top seam, form a triangle shape. Stitch across the triangle at right angles 1in/2.5cm from the point. Test the fit.

16 Sew the pressed hems on the sides of the openings. Press a 2in/5cm double hem on all lower edges.

17 Add grommets through the hems following the instructions on page 93.

18 Sew the ties, following the instructions for the *Cushioned Chair Seat Cover*.

cushioned chair back & seat covers

◆

This chair back cover is quite simply a padded rectangle that folds in half over the chair back. The idea can be adapted for most chairs.

MATERIALS

- ◆ *Orange cotton-and-linen blend*
- ◆ *Yellow cotton-and-linen blend*
- ◆ *Batting*
- ◆ *Sewing kit*

1 For ties, from yellow, cut eight strips 2½ x 16in/6.5 x 40.75cm. Cut four from orange. Press in a seam at the short ends. Press in ½in/1.5cm along each long edge. Fold in half lengthways and press. Stitch around the ties.

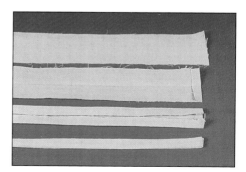

2 Make a paper template of the chair seat. Cut two from fabric ¾in/2cm larger all around. Cut one shape from batting slightly smaller than the template.

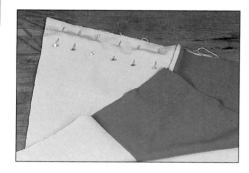

3 Position the ties on the right side of the back edge of each cushion 2–3in/5–7.5cm from the sides. Pin. Center the batting on the wrong side of the cushion front. Baste together.

4 Place the back and front right sides together and pin. Begin stitching 4in/10cm from one corner of the back of the cushion, catching the ties in the stitching. Leave a gap at the center back.

5 Turn the cushion right side out through the gap. Hand-stitch the gap.

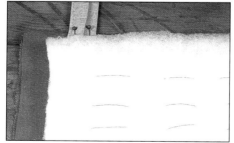

6 Make a template of the shape of both sides of the chair back. Cut one shape from orange for the wrong side, adding ¾in/2cm all around. Cut one shape from batting slightly smaller than the template. For the cushion front divide the template into four. Cut two sections from orange and two from yellow, adding ¾in/2cm seams all around.

7 Stitch together the orange and yellow pieces to form the cushion front.

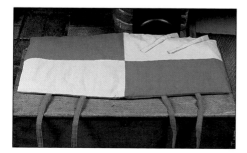

8 Make up the cushion following the instructions at steps 3–5. Insert the ties at convenient points at each side of the cushion and tie each around the sides of the chair.

folding picnic stool

◆

Made for a stool with a center-side opening. If replacing a worn-out seat, use the old cover as your template.

Adapt the measurements to fit your own stool

MATERIALS

◆ *Red-and-orange striped fabric*
◆ *Sewing kit*
◆ *Stool frame*
◆ *Silver paint*

1 Using silver paint, paint the framework of a stool.

2 Determine the width and depth of the chair seat required. Add to your measurement 1in/2.5cm to the front and back for turnings. Add 4in/10cm to each side. Cut the fabric to your requirements.

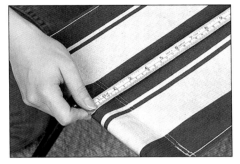

3 At the front and back, turn under ½in/1.5cm, then another ½in/1.5cm. Press and stitch to hold.

4 At each side turn under 1¼in/3cm. Press. Machine-stitch to hold. Turn under another 2½in/6.5cm and machine-stitch close to the folded edge, leaving maximum room for the bars of the stool.

index

112 ◀